W9-DHW-150

Playmakers

Catchers

Tom Greve

ROURKE PUBLISHING
Vero Beach, Florida 32964

www.rourkepublishing.com

PHOTO CREDITS: © Marc Julagay: Title Page; © Donald Linscott: 5; © Philip Lange: 6; © Ana Abejon: 6; © Associated Press: 7, 11, 12, 13, 16, 17; © jtroudt: 9; © David Freund: 14; © Joseph Abbott: 15; © Rob Friedman: 18; © Kenneth Mellott: 19; © Jared Matson: 20; © Dennis Oblander: 21; © Wendy Nero: 22

Editor: Jeanne Sturm

Cover and page design by Tara Raymo

Library of Congress Cataloging-in-Publication Data

Greve, Tom.
  Catchers / Tom Greve.
     p. cm. -- (Playmakers)
  Includes index.
  ISBN 978-1-60694-329-8 (hard cover)
  ISBN 978-1-60694-828-6 (soft cover)
 1. Catching (Baseball)--Juvenile literature. 2. Catchers (Baseball)--United States--Biography--Juvenile literature. I. Title.
  GV872.G74 2010
  796.357'23--dc22

                                           2009006018

Printed in the USA

CG/CG

ROURKE PUBLISHING

www.rourkepublishing.com - rourke@rourkepublishing.com
Post Office Box 643328 Vero Beach, Florida 32964

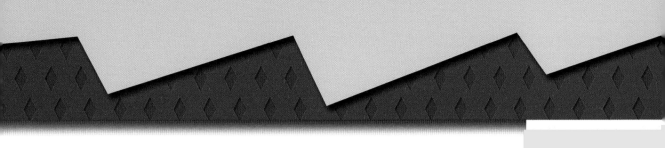

Table of Contents

Catchers

No player on a baseball team has a tougher job than the catcher. Catchers have to catch hard-thrown balls from the pitcher. They have to wear protective padding and a catcher's mask. They also have to **squat** behind the **plate** for most of the game and sometimes endure collisions with base runners trying to score. OUCH!

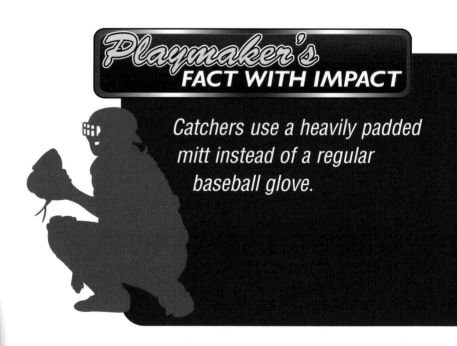

Playmaker's FACT WITH IMPACT

Catchers use a heavily padded mitt instead of a regular baseball glove.

A catcher's main jobs on defense are to catch pitches, keep **wild pitches** from getting past them, and throwing out base runners trying to **steal.**

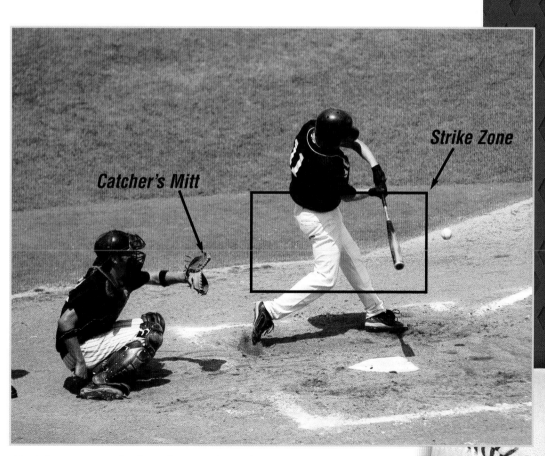

Catcher's Mitt

Strike Zone

Catchers use their mitt to give the pitcher a target in the strike zone.

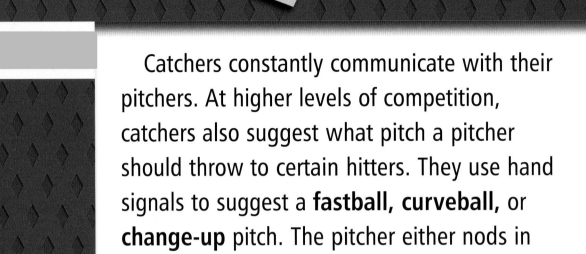

Catchers constantly communicate with their pitchers. At higher levels of competition, catchers also suggest what pitch a pitcher should throw to certain hitters. They use hand signals to suggest a **fastball, curveball,** or **change-up** pitch. The pitcher either nods in agreement or asks for another suggestion.

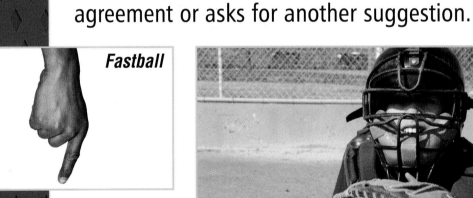

Fastball

Curveball

Change-up

*When teams do well, some of the credit goes to the catcher for his **rapport** with the pitching staff.*

Ivan Rodriguez is perhaps the best catcher currently playing in the major leagues.

GREATS of the GAME

*Nicknamed Pudge, Ivan Rodriguez has played for Texas, Florida, Detroit, and the New York Yankees during his career. He won the Most Valuable Player awards in both the American and National Leagues. His career **batting average** is .301.*

Skills Behind the Plate

In addition to catching balls, catchers also have to throw. When a player from the other team tries to steal a base, the catcher must throw the ball to second or third base before the runner arrives to prevent a stolen base. When a catcher does this, it's called throwing out a base runner.

Playmaker's FACT WITH IMPACT

Other than batting average on offense, one of the most important statistics for a catcher is his defensive stolen base percentage. This measures a catcher's throwing ability to stop the other team from stealing bases, vital in making it more difficult for them to score.

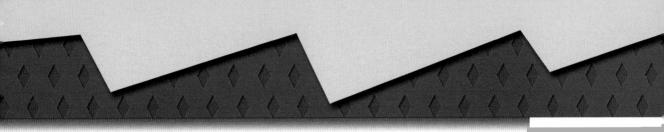

Catchers often have among the strongest throwing arms on the entire team.

Catchers need tremendous **coordination** between their hands and eyes. Catching a 95 mile per hour (153 kilometer per hour) fastball is not easy.

They also need quick **reflexes.** When a batter hits a ball straight up in the air, the catcher must pop out of his squat position, throw off his mask, find the ball in the air, and catch it before it hits the ground.

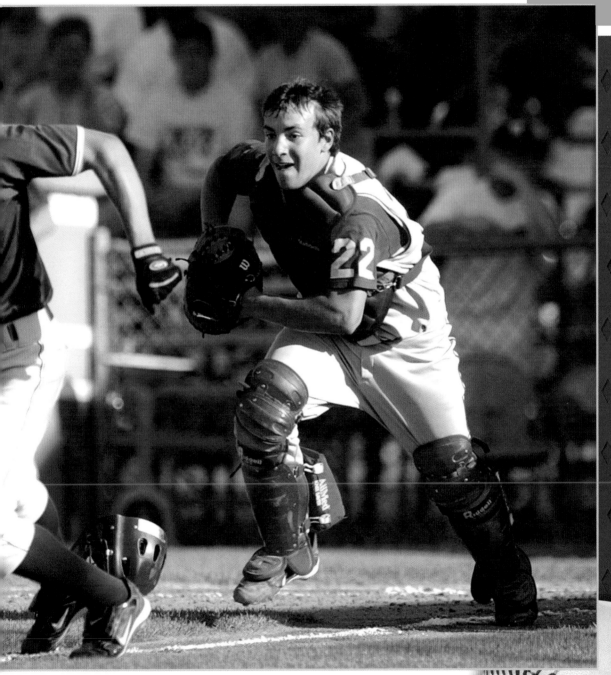

The mask protects the catcher's head, face, and eyes, but once the ball is in play, he can toss it aside to see better.

Hall-of-Famer Johnny Bench won ten Gold Glove awards for outstanding defensive play for the Cincinnati Reds.

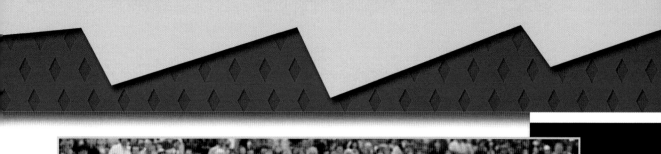

Johnny Bench was National League Rookie of the Year in 1968, won two Most Valuable Player awards, and appeared in 12 All-Star games during his career. His team, the Reds, won the World Series twice. In addition to his outstanding defense, he also managed to hit 389 career home runs.

Dangers Behind the Plate

Playing catcher can be dangerous. At the college or professional level, it means catching pitches thrown at nearly 100 miles per hour (161 kilometers per hour). Sometimes catchers have to throw their bodies in front of pitches that bounce off the ground in front of them. To avoid injury or pain, catchers have to wear numerous pieces of protective equipment.

Catcher's Mask

Chest Protector

Shin Guards

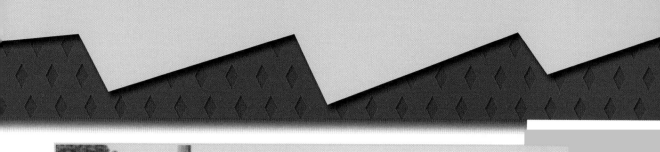

With their masks, chest protectors, and shin guards, catchers prepare for the impact of the ball—or another player.

Since catchers have such a hard job on defense, they are not usually among a team's best batters. Catchers with batting averages over .300 are rare, and valuable to their team.

Despite the physical toll of the position, Mike Piazza became perhaps the greatest hitting catcher of all time.

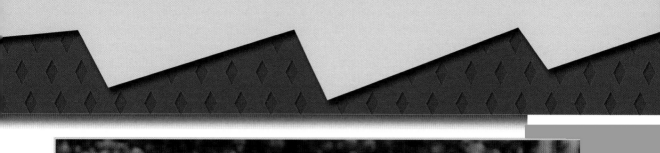

GREATS of the GAME

Mike Piazza won the National League Rookie of the Year award in 1988. Over the course of his 15-year career, he hit 427 home runs, more than any other catcher. His career batting average was .308. He played most of his career with the Los Angeles Dodgers and New York Mets. He retired in 2008 after appearing in twelve All-Star games.

So You Want to Be a Catcher?

Prepare for Impact! Catchers have the most physically demanding job on a baseball team. They have to be willing to use their bodies to block pitches, and sometimes even base runners.

By squatting, the catcher stays level with the strike zone.

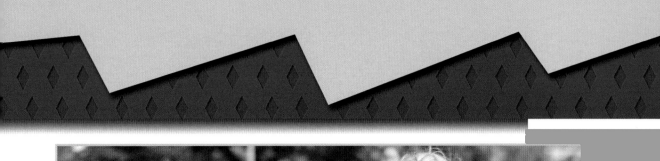

Part of the catcher's job is to defend home plate like the other infielders defend their bases.

Here comes the throw! One of the most exciting plays in baseball is a close play at home plate. This involves a base runner trying to score as the catcher tries to catch a throw and tag him out. The umpire calls the runner safe or out. Either way, the catcher often gets run over.

Catchers play just in front of the home plate umpire. It is important for them to avoid arguing that a pitch was a strike when the umpire ruled it a ball. The catcher can ask questions of the umpire, but it should be in a respectful manner.

The umpire peers over the catcher's shoulder to get the best view of the strike zone so he can call balls and strikes.

When a pitcher struggles, the catcher and team manager can come to the mound for a quick strategy chat.

Catchers have the hardest job of all the players on a baseball team. They need to catch and throw well, and be willing to get hit by pitches, and by the other team's base runners.

If you like playing catch and don't mind getting some bumps and bruises, then grab a mask and some padding. You might be ready to start learning how to be a catcher.

Glossary

batting average (BA-ting AV-uh-rij): number that reflects how frequently batters succeed in hitting the ball and reaching base safely

change-up (CHAYNJ-uhp): a pitch thrown slower than previous pitches

coordination (koh-OR-duh-nay-shuhn): the ability to perform several physical tasks at the same time

curveball (KURV-bawl): a pitch that curves slightly as it moves toward the catcher

fastball (FAST-bawl): a pitch thrown as hard as possible

plate (PLAYT): another name for home base

rapport (ruh-POR): relationship or understanding between teammates

reflexes (REE-fleks-ez): a person's ability to move or react

squat (SKWAHT): in a crouched position with knees bent

steal (STEEL): run to the next base as the pitcher throws toward the catcher

wild pitches (WILDE PICH-ez): throws from pitchers, which badly miss their target

Index

Websites to Visit

www.baseballcatchers.com
www.baseball-catcher.com
www.qcbaseball.com/skills/catching1.aspx

About the Author

Tom Greve lives in Chicago with his wife, Meg, and their two children, Madison and William. He enjoys playing, watching, and writing about sports.